The History of Early New York

Jeremy Thornton

The Rosen Publishing Group's
PowerKids Press™
New York

For my daughter, Ainsley Sarah

Published in 2003 by The Rosen Publishing Group, Inc.
29 East 21st Street, New York, NY 10010

First Edition

Editor: Joanne Randolph
Designers: Michael J. Caroleo, Mike Donnellan, Michael de Guzman, Colin Dizengoff
Layout: Nick Sciacca

Photo Credits: Cover, p. 19 © Collection of The New-York Historical Society/57812; pp. 4, 11 © North Wind Picture Archives; pp. 7, 8 (inset), p 20 (left) © Bettmann/CORBIS; p. 8 © New York State Library; p. 12 (left) © Collection of The New-York Historical Society/73871; p. 12 (top) cat. no. 20.0/1795, (bottom) cat. no. 20.1/6541 © American Museum of Natural History; p. 15 © Collection of The New-York Historical Society/1909.2; p. 16 © SuperStock; p. 20 (right) © CORBIS.

Thornton, Jeremy.
The history of early New York / Jeremy Thornton.
    p. cm. — (Building America's democracy)
Includes bibliographical references (p.) and index.
  ISBN 0-8239-6278-4 (library binding)
    1. New York (N.Y.)—History—Colonial period, ca. 1600–1775—Juvenile literature. [1. New York (N.Y.)—History—Colonial period, ca. 1600–1775.] I. Title.
    F128.4 .T48 2003
    974.7'102—dc21

                                        2001006662

Manufactured in the United States of America

Contents

The Algonquians

Native Americans were the first people who lived in what is now New York. In fact, Manhattan, part of New York City, got its name from the Algonquian nation's word for this island, *Manna-hatta*, which means "island of the hills." The Algonquians were skilled hunters and fishers. They traveled all around the island in canoes. They trapped small animals for their furs. The women farmed corn, pumpkins, squash, and beans. They gathered apples, peaches, grapes, and other fruit. The Algonquians were governed by leaders whom they called *sachems*. In all there were several hundred Algonquians living on the island when the first **explorers** from Europe came to the North American continent and to New York.

Explorers who arrived in New York and sailed up the Hudson River probably saw Algonquian and Iroquois villages like this one, with longhouses or wigwams.

European Explorers

The first European to see New York was Giovanni da Verrazano, in 1524. He was an Italian explorer sent by the king of France to look for a route to China. He stayed in America only long enough to explore the island of Manhattan, and then he returned to France. He told the French king about the people he saw in canoes. In 1609, Henry Hudson sailed to New York **harbor** in his ship, the *Half Moon*. He worked for a trading company called the Dutch East India Company. Hudson traded with the Algonquians, giving them cloth, metal tools, and **trinkets** in return for furs and tobacco. This was the beginning of **widespread** European trade with the Native Americans.

This is Henry Hudson's ship, the *Half Moon*, in which he explored the Hudson River in the 1600s. The *Half Moon* was originally commissioned on March 25, 1609.

The Dutch Buy Manhattan

The Dutch decided to create a settlement for traders on the southern tip of Manhattan. They sent settlers to form the new colony. In 1626, Peter Minuit was made **director-general** of the colony. He wanted an agreement with the Algonquians that would give the Dutch the right to use the land. He called the sachems to a meeting and paid them in goods for the land on which the Dutch would build the settlement. Legend has it Minuit bought the island for $24 worth of trinkets. This has never been proven. Also, the goods, such as metal tools, that were traded would have been quite valuable to the Algonquians. However, the Algonquians thought the Dutch were just going to use the land for a short time. This led to problems later.

For many years, historians believed this deed for Manhattan was real, but it was later proven to be a fake. *Inset:* Peter Minuit was born in Germany in 1580.

New Amsterdam

New Amsterdam is what the Dutch called the settlement that they formed on Manhattan. It served as the **capital** of the larger Dutch colony, New Netherland. They built walls around the settlement to protect it from attack. They dug a **canal** so that they could sail into the colony and unload ships. They built a fort, houses, a **tavern**, a church, and even an **inn**. The most important building, the only building made of stone, was the counting house. Furs and money belonging to the Dutch East India Company were kept there. Some of the settlers were farmers, some were shipbuilders, and some were merchants who traded with the Algonquians.

This hand-colored woodcut shows the landing of the first European settlers in New Amsterdam in the 1600s. This first group was made up of 110 people.

Life in the Colony

The fur trade was very successful. The Dutch brought goods, such as metal tools, from Europe to give to the Algonquians. The Dutch traded for the furs of beavers, otters, minks, and other animals, which they sent back to Europe. However, there were problems. The Dutch settlers began to steal from one another. They **smuggled** furs so that they wouldn't have to pay taxes. There was crime and drunkenness on the streets. When the Algonquians realized that the Dutch were not going to give the land back to them, they began to fight with the settlers. The Algonquians were not happy that more and more settlers were coming to live in the colony and were taking even more land from them.

Beaver skins and metal tools, such as axes and kettles, were just a few of the valuable items that were traded between the Dutch settlers and the Algonquians.

Peter Stuyvesant

Peter Stuyvesant became director-general of New Netherland in 1647. His job was to solve the problems in the colony. He had been the director of Dutch colonies in the **Caribbean**. While there, he had lost a leg in a battle with the Spanish, and he wore a wooden leg in its place. He was a very **stern** man with a quick temper. He tried to make New Amsterdam a better place. He tried to stop smuggling and crime. He made it illegal to fight or to let animals wander in the streets. He punished settlers when they stole or cheated. He taxed alcohol. He also worked to fix up the fort. He wanted to protect the colony from attack by Native Americans and other colonies, such as those of Sweden and Britain.

During his time as director-general of New Netherland, Peter Stuyvesant became a legend because of his quick temper and the strict rules he forced on the settlers.

The English Take Over

New Netherland was a valuable piece of land because of its location and its natural resources. There had been battles between the Algonquians and the Dutch about the ownership of the land for many years. There had also been problems with New Sweden. The English also wanted to control the Dutch colony. In 1664, the king of England, Charles II, gave New Netherland to his brother, James, the duke of York. The king then sent four warships to take the island from the Dutch. Peter Stuyvesant wanted to fight, but the Dutch colonists signed a **petition** asking Stuyvesant to **surrender**. They were tired of fighting. Stuyvesant gave in and surrendered. The English renamed the colony New York in honor of the duke.

Stuyvesant surrendered New Netherland on September 5, 1664. The Dutch were allowed to keep their homes and most of the rights they had enjoyed under Dutch rule.

Growth of New York

New York grew richer under English rule. The British navy was the largest navy in the world. British merchant ships, which were protected by the navy, traveled all over the globe. They carried furs and other goods between Europe and the Americas. The harbor at Manhattan was protected from bad weather and was easy to get into and out of. There were many places for ships to sail into, making it a perfect port. This made New York, and especially Manhattan, an important center for trade and shipping. Many people came to live in New York, and the population of Manhattan grew quickly. By 1775, there were about 26,000 people living in New York City.

This is how Manhattan looked in 1660, near the time when Britain took over. All of the colonists lived at the island's tip. The city would grow rapidly over the next century.

Revolution

After an expensive war against the French, called the French and Indian War (1754–1763), the king of England decided to tax the American colonies. In New York and the other colonies, many people hated the taxes imposed on them by acts like the Stamp Act (1764) and the Tea Act (1773). On April 19, 1775, the **American Revolution** began. The people of New York joined the other colonies in the fight for independence from Britain. In fact the Declaration of Independence was first read aloud in New York City. The British soon **defeated** George Washington's troops in New York City. The British used the city as a military base until the colonists won the war in 1783.

Left: This is a plan of Manhattan as the island appeared in 1755. *Right:* This cartoon shows a tax collector being tarred and feathered by patriots angry over the Tea Act.

New York Today

After the war, New York City was made the first capital of the newly formed United States of America. General George Washington, the first president of the United States, lived in New York City until the capital was moved to Washington, D.C. New York City continued to grow, and it quickly became the largest city in the United States. Today it is a center of **industry**, trade, **culture**, and art. It has become one of the most important cities in the world. It is a **symbol** of freedom and success to people all over the globe.

Glossary

American Revolution (uh-MER-uh-ken reh-vuh-LOO-shun) Battles that soldiers from the American colonies fought against England for freedom.

canal (kuh-NAL) A waterway dug across land for ships to go through or to carry water to places that need it.

capital (KA-pih-tul) The place where the government for a certain area is located.

Caribbean (kar-uh-BEE-uhn) A part of the Atlantic Ocean that is bounded by the West Indies, South America, and Central America.

culture (KUL-cher) The beliefs, customs, art, and religions of a group of people.

defeated (dih-FEET-ed) To have won against someone in a contest or battle.

director-general (dih-REK-tur JEN-rul) The head of local government in the Dutch colonies.

explorers (ik-SPLOR-urz) People who travel for adventure or discovery.

harbor (HAR-bor) A protected body of water where ships anchor.

industry (IN-dus-tree) The large-scale production of goods for profit.

inn (IN) A place that provides food and lodging for travelers.

petition (puh-TIH-shun) A written request signed by many people.

smuggled (SMUH-guld) Transported goods illegally and secretly.

stern (STERN) Harsh and severe in personality.

surrender (suh-REN-der) To give up.

symbol (SIM-bul) A person, an object, or a design that stands for something important.

tavern (TA-vurn) A place of business where alcohol is sold.

trinkets (TRINK-its) Small, cheap objects.

widespread (WYD-spred) Large-scale, reaching over a large area.

Index

Primary Sources

Page 7: Held by the New-York Historical Society, this is an accurate model of Henry Hudson's ship, the *Half Moon*, or *Halve Maen*. The model was created between 1825 and 1900, using wood, metal, canvas, paint, and string. **Page 8:** The engraved portrait of Peter Minuit was created in the 1600s. The forged deed was found in the 1920s. It took many years for it to be proven as a fake. It is now held at the New-York Historical Society. No real deed has ever been found. **Page 12:** The beaver pelt is held at the New-York Historical Society. The pelts were stretched on wooden frames like this as part of the tanning process used to soften animal hides into leather. Metal axheads and brass kettles like these, held at the Museum of Natural History, were typical items that might have been used by the Dutch in trade with the Indians. **Page 15:** This oil painting, held by the New-York Historical Society, was painted by Henri Couturier between 1660 and 1663 on a wood panel. **Page 16:** *The Fall of New Amsterdam, 1664* was painted by Jean Leon Gerome Ferris. Gerome Ferris studied with his father, S. J. Ferris, a notable artist in Philadelphia. He also studied in Paris with Gerome Bougereau. He was a member of the Artist Fund in Philadelphia and the Society of Etchers in Philadelphia. In 1900, he began his series of paintings on American History. The Museum of Independence Hall houses a collection of more than 70 canvases. His work is also held by the Natural History Museum in New York and the New-York Historical Society. **Page 19:** This redraft of the Costello Plan, showing New Amsterdam in 1660, was done by John Wolcott Adams and published by I. N. Phelps Stokes in 1916. This map is held at the New-York Historical Society. **Page 20:** The map, drawn by B. Ratzen between 1766 and 1767, is a plan of New York City based on his own surveys and those done in 1755 by F. Maerschalck, the city surveyor. The print by D. C. Johnston, entitled *The Bostonians Paying the Exciseman or Tarring and Feathering*, was published in London in 1774. This kind of satirical cartoon was quite common at that time. Here the Liberty Tree stands in the background with the Stamp Act tacked upside down on the trunk. Tea is being dumped in the background as patriots pour tea into the mouth of a taxman who has been tarred and feathered.

Web Sites

Due to the changing nature of Internet links, PowerKids Press has developed an online list of Web sites related to the subject of this book. This site is updated regularly. Please use this link to access the list:

www.powerkidslinks.com/bad/hiseny